STARS OF SPORTS

PATRICK MAHOMES

FOOTBALL MVP

by Matt Chandler

CAPSTONE PRESS
a capstone imprint

Stars of Sports is published by
Capstone Press, an imprint of Capstone
1710 Roe Crest Drive, North Mankato, Minnesota 56003
www.capstonepub.com

**Library of Congress Cataloging-in-Publication Data is available on the Library
of Congress website.**
978-1-5435-9175-0 (library binding)
978-1-5435-9188-0 (eBook PDF)

Summary: Patrick Mahomes, the 2018 most valuable player in the National Football
League, could have succeeded in any sport. Growing up, he played baseball,
basketball, and football. After joining the Kansas City Chiefs in the NFL, he broke
record after record, including most passing yards and most passes completed in
a single season. Learn all the facts on Mahomes's meteoric rise in the NFL in this
exciting biography.

Editorial Credits
Editor: Hank Musolf; Designer: Ashlee Suker; Media Researcher: Eric Gohl;
Production Specialist: Laura Manthe

Image Credits
Associated Press: Colin Braley, 27, Icon Sportswire/Sam Grenadier, 13, Kathy
Willens, 6, Tyler Morning Telegraph/Chelsea Purgahn, 15, Tyler Morning Telegraph/
Victor Texcucano, 8, 9; Newscom: Cal Sport Media/Jevone Moore, 21, Icon
Sportswire/Kevin French, 12, Icon Sportswire/Scott Winters, cover, 5, 23, TNS/John
Sleezer, 16, USA Today Sports/Dale Zanine, 24, USA Today Sports/Denny Medley,
19, ZUMA Press/Hector Acevedo, 17; Shutterstock: Aspen Photo, 11, Jamie Lamor
Thompson, 28, Stuart Monk, 1

All internet sites appearing in back matter were available and accurate when this
book was sent to press.

Printed in the United States of America.
PA99

TABLE OF CONTENTS

Glossary terms are **BOLD** on first use.

A RECORD PASS

Patrick Mahomes dropped back to pass. The Kansas City Chiefs' quarterback stepped up. He got in position in the pocket. He tossed the ball downfield. The wide receiver made the grab. He raced to the end zone. Mahomes had thrown his 50th touchdown pass during the 2018 season. He was only 23 years old!

2018 was Mahomes' first season as a starting quarterback in the National Football League (NFL). Only two other quarterbacks had thrown 50 touchdowns in a season. Will Patrick Mahomes end up in the NFL **Hall of Fame?** For now, he has earned his place in the record books.

Mahomes makes a pass against the Oakland Raiders in 2018. 〉〉〉

CHAPTER ONE

BEFORE THE FAME

Patrick Mahomes was born in Tyler, Texas, on September 17, 1995. He grew up around sports. His dad was a baseball pitcher. Patrick met Derek Jeter and Alex Rodriguez. He chased fly balls on the field before the 2000 World Series.

His dad wanted Patrick to follow his path. He wanted Patrick to play baseball. Patrick played three sports in high school. He played baseball, football, and basketball. At 6 foot 3 inches (192 centimeters) tall, he was a natural athlete.

⟨⟨⟨ A young Mahomes gets ready to catch a baseball.

Baseball Star

Today Mahomes is a football star. But in school he was known for baseball. As a pitcher in high school, Mahomes threw a **no-hitter** for his baseball team. He struck out 16 hitters. He was a good hitter too.

7

HIGH SCHOOL SUPERSTAR

By 2013, Mahomes had great skill in basketball, baseball, and football. But it was football that stole the show. Mahomes passed for 4,619 yards in 2013. He ran with the football, or **rushed,** for 940 more. Mahomes scored 65 touchdowns in a single season! He was named the Texas State Football Player of the Year in 2013.

〉〉〉 Mahomes posed for a picture with his family after receiving the player of the year award.

>>> Mahomes rushes against the Carthage Bulldogs in 2013.

Then Mahomes made a tough choice. He gave up basketball. He wanted to focus on football. Mahomes decided to go to Texas Tech University. He wanted to play football and baseball there.

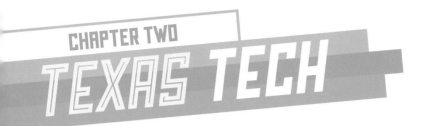
Texas Tech's football team is the Red Raiders. Mahomes was named their starter quarterback. They played against Sam Houston State in the first game of the season. Mahomes completed 33 passes for 425 yards in the game. He tossed four touchdowns in a 59-45 win. For Texas Tech fans, things were about to get better!

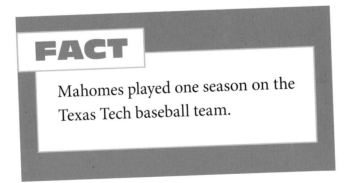

FACT

Mahomes played one season on the Texas Tech baseball team.

>>> Mahomes speeds ahead in a 2015 game.

BREAKOUT SEASON

Mahomes' junior year at Texas Tech had both good and bad parts. The team finished with a losing record of 5-7, but Mahomes had a great season. He threw for 5,052 yards and 41 touchdowns.

‹‹‹ Mahomes drops back in a game against Arizona State.

>>> Mahomes throws on the run in a 2016 game.

On October 22, 2016, he earned another record. Texas Tech faced off against Oklahoma. Mahomes was taking on another future NFL star. That player was Baker Mayfield. The two teams combined for 125 points. Mahomes had the biggest game of his life. He attempted 88 passes in the game, one short of a record. He scored five touchdowns. Mahomes rushed for 85 yards in the game.

CHAPTER THREE

DRAFT DAY

At the end of the 2016 season, Mahomes had a tough choice to make. He could stay at Texas Tech. He would have one more season there. There was also the chance to leave college. Leaving college could mean a shot at the NFL.

On January 3, 2017, Mahomes made his decision. He said he would enter the NFL draft. The Chiefs wanted Mahomes. He was the second quarterback chosen in the draft. He was a Kansas City Chief!

>>> Mahomes after being drafted by the Kansas City Chiefs on April 27, 2017.

FIRST-ROUND BACKUP

Mahomes worked as backup quarterback. Fans in Kansas City wanted to see the **rookie** play. They got their wish for the last game of the season. Mahomes got his first NFL start. He led his team to a 27-24 win against their **division** rivals, the Denver Broncos.

>>> Mahomes (left) looks on at the bench as backup quarterback.

>>> Mahomes in his first NFL start against the Broncos

CHAPTER FOUR
NFL STARTER

The Chiefs were first in their division in 2017. Mahomes was the starter quarterback in 2018. Mahomes wanted to lead his new team to the playoffs. He threw 10 touchdown passes in his first two games of the season.

Mahomes and his team won the first six games. He averaged 31 touchdown passes per season in college. For many players, the jump to playing pro games can be difficult. Not for Mahomes. He set the NFL on fire with 50 touchdown passes in his first season as a starter.

Mahomes threw touchdown passes in 15 of the Chiefs' 16 regular-season games. He threw four or more touchdowns during seven games. He joined Steelers' quarterback Ben Roethlisberger as the only quarterback to have two six-touchdown games in the same season.

>>> Mahomes throws as Matthew Judon of the Broncos closes in.

Mahomes added two more rushing touchdowns in the regular season. In 2018 he scored 56 touchdowns in all!

FACT

Mahomes is right-handed. In 2018, Mahomes completed a pass left-handed! He was being sacked by Von Miller. Mahomes switched hands and dumped the ball to Tyrek Hill for a first down.

GAME-SAVING THROW

The biggest home win for Mahomes came on December 9. It was against the Baltimore Ravens. A win would get the Chiefs a playoff spot. The Chiefs trailed 24-17. Less than two minutes were left to go in the game. Mahomes flung the ball downfield. Tyrek Hill made a game-saving 50-yard grab. The Chiefs scored and won the game. Mahomes had led his team back to the playoffs!

A Thrilling Showdown

Mahomes led the Chiefs to nine wins in the first 10 games of 2018. Then came a showdown against the Los Angeles Rams on November 19. The 23-year-old quarterback threw for 478 yards and ran for 28 more. He threw six touchdowns. He led his team to 51 points. The Rams won the game 54-51. But Patrick Mahomes had an amazing game.

Mahomes points out a linebacker in a 2018 game.

FACT

Mahomes can throw the ball incredibly far!
During warmups in 2018, he threw the ball
90 yards. He made it look easy!

THE PLAYOFFS

Mahomes led the Chiefs to a division win in 2018. Could he lead his team to a home playoff win against the Indianapolis Colts?

In his first career playoff drive, Mahomes drove the Chiefs 90 yards down the field. Snow fell over the field. They scored a touchdown and took a 7-0 lead. They never trailed in the game and beat the Colts 31-13.

The Chiefs were one win away from the Super Bowl. Mahomes would have to outplay five-time Super Bowl Champion Tom Brady in the American Football Conference (AFC) Championship Game.

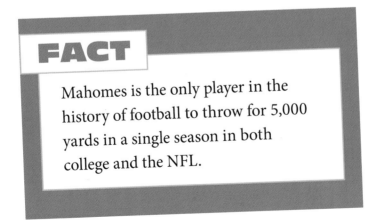

FACT

Mahomes is the only player in the history of football to throw for 5,000 yards in a single season in both college and the NFL.

There were 32 seconds left in the game. The Chiefs trailed 31-28. Mahomes connected on two quick passes. He had his team in field goal range. The kicker nailed a 39-yard kick to send the game to overtime. The Patriots won the game, 37-31. Mahomes finished the game with 295 passing yards and three touchdowns. He showed he could compete with the best players in the game.

⟩⟩⟩ Mahomes stiff-arms Patrick Chung of the Patriots.

Mahomes posed with ›››
the MVP award on
February 2, 2019.

CHAPTER FIVE

MVP WINNER

Mahomes was just 23 years old when he won the 2018 Most Valuable Player (MVP) award. Mahomes crushed a lot of records in 2018. He had a lot to be proud of. He led the league in passing touchdowns. He was the second leading Chiefs rusher. The Chiefs had only played in one AFC Championship Game in 48 years. Patrick Mahomes took them back to the title game.

Mahomes threw touchdown passes to 12 different players in 2018. Four of his offensive teammates made the Pro Bowl with him. The top players of the season play together in this big game. Patrick was chosen by fans, coaches, and other players to be on a Pro Bowl team.

FACT

Mahomes talked about his love for ketchup during a 2018 interview. He got an **endorsement** deal with TV ads from Heinz, a company that makes ketchup.

OFF-FIELD SUCCESS

Mahomes is focused on being the best player he can be. Off the field, he stays busy too. Mahomes works to help the community of Kansas City. During the 2018 season, Mahomes visited patients at the University of Kansas hospital. He also worked as a volunteer with the **Veterans** Community Project. The group builds homes for homeless veterans.

Mahomes also helps young people in his community. He works with a group called KC United. The group provides support and opportunities for kids. Members help kids join football, basketball, and other sports teams.

Mahomes took children shopping for KC United. 〉〉〉

ANY TEAM, ANY TIME, ANYWHERE
SHOP YOUR FAVORITE TEAMS' LICENSED GEAR 24/7

DICKS.COM

LOOKING AHEAD

What will the future bring for Patrick Mahomes? He already has a league MVP trophy. He has led his team deep into the playoffs. Best of all, he's still very young. Patrick Mahomes is just 24. Fans and players are excited for what's next. Experts think he can only get better. Mahomes says his one goal in the future is winning the Super Bowl. Fans in Kansas City hope the future includes Mahomes holding up many trophies!

⟨⟨⟨ Mahomes at a 2019 festival

TIMELINE

1995 born on September 17 in Tyler, Texas

2014 throws a no-hitter for his high school baseball team in Whitehouse, Texas

2016 sets NCAA single-game records with 734 yards passing and 819 yards of total offense

2016 receives the Sammy Baugh Trophy as the best passer in college football

2017 selected as the 10th pick in the first round of the NFL Draft by the Kansas City Chiefs

2018 becomes the starting Chiefs quarterback

2018 sets NFL record as first quarterback to throw for more than 3,000 yards in first 10 career starts (3,185) on November 4

2019 named league MVP on February 2 for the 2018 season

GLOSSARY

DIVISION (duh-VI-zhuhn)—a group of people or teams in a certain category for a competition

ENDORSEMENT (in-DORS-muhnt)—the act of an athlete wearing, promoting, or using a product, often times for money

HALL OF FAME (HAL of FAYM)—a place where important people are honored

NATIVE (NAY-tuhv)—someone who was born in a particular country or place

NO-HITTER (no-HIT-ur)—a game in which one team doesn't allow the other team to get a hit

POCKET (POK-it)—the area behind the offensive line from which a quarterback usually throws passes

PRO BOWL (PROH BOWL)—the NFL's All-Star Game in which the top players in the American Football Conference play against those from the National Football Conference (NFC)

VETERAN (VET-ur-uhns)—a former member of the military

READ MORE

Chandler, Matt. *Football: A Guide for Players and Fans.* North Mankato, MN: Capstone Press, 2019.

Graves, Will. *Football's New Wave: The Young Superstars Taking Over the Game.* Mendota Heights, MN: North Star Editions, 2019.

Rogers, Andy. *Who's Who of Pro Football: A Guide to the Game's Greatest Players.* North Mankato, MN: Capstone Press, 2016.

INTERNET SITES

Kansas City Chiefs
www.chiefs.com

The National Football League
www.nfl.com

Pro Football Hall of Fame
www.profootballhof.com

INDEX